Oil Spills

by Christine A. Caputo

Consultant:
Ian R. MacDonald
Professor of Oceanography
Florida State University

Raintree

www.raintreepublishers.co.uk
Visit our website to find out more information about Raintree books.

To order:
☎ Phone 0845 6044371
🖷 Fax +44 (0) 1865 312263
🖳 Email myorders@raintreepublishers.co.uk

Customers from outside the UK please telephone +44 1865 312262

Raintree is an imprint of Capstone Global Library Limited, a company incorporated in England and Wales having its registered office at 7 Pilgrim Street, London, EC4V 6LB – Registered company number: 6695582

Senior Art Director: Rahul Dhiman
Art Director: Joita Das
Editor: John-Paul Wilkins
Designer: Marish Kumar
Illustrator: Bibin Jose
Picture Research: Akansha Srivastava
Originated by Capstone Global Library Ltd
Printed and bound in China by Leo Paper Products Ltd

ISBN 978 1 406 23009 3 (hardback)
15 14 13 12 11
10 9 8 7 6 5 4 3 2 1

ISBN 978 1 406 23010 9 (paperback)
15 14 13 12 11
10 9 8 7 6 5 4 3 2 1

British Library Cataloguing in Publication Data
Caputo, Christine A., 1966-
  Oil spills.
363.7'382-dc22
A full catalogue record for this book is available from the British Library.

Acknowledgements
t= top, b=bottom, l=left, r=right, c=centre
Cover page: Michel Gunther/Bios/Photolibrary.
Title page: Wimclaes/Dreamstime.
4: Dmitriy Shironosov/Shutterstock; 4–5: Ssuaphotos/Shutterstock; 6–7: Frontpage/Shutterstock; 6: Martin Leigh/Oxford Scientific (OSF)/Photolibrary; 8: Banol2007/Dreamstime; 9: Danny E Hooks/Shutterstock; 10-11: Wimclaes/Dreamstime; 12-13: Kent Wohl/ US Fish and Wildlife Service; 14-15: U.S. Coast Guard photo; 16: Patrick Nichols/ U.S. Gulf Coast/U.S. Navy photo; 17: Petty Officer 3rd Class Walter Shinn/ U.S. Coast Guard photo; 18-19: U.S. Coast Guard photo; 20l: Petty Officer 3rd Class Colin White/ U.S. Coast Guard photo; 20r: Petty Officer 3rd Class Nathan W. Bradshaw/U.S. Coast Guard photo; 21l: Petty Officer 1st Class Krystyna Hannum/U.S. Coast Guard photo; 21r: Petty Officer 3rd Class Robert Brazzell/U.S. Coast Guard photo
Q2AMedia Art Bank: 12, 15

Contents

Oil and earth

Where does petrol come from? What is used to make both electricity and plastic? The answer is oil.

Oil found below Earth's surface is known as **petroleum**. It is formed from tiny plants that lived in the oceans millions of years ago. Oil is one of our most valuable **natural resources**.

OIL FACT

The word "petroleum" comes from two Latin words meaning "rock" and "oil".

petroleum thick, oily liquid found below
Earth's surface

natural resource material people use that
is found in nature

5

Oil and water

Pour oil into water, and watch what happens. The oil floats on top! It is easy to see that oil and water don't mix. Oil and water don't mix in nature, either.

An **oil spill** is when oil accidently gets into the **environment**. Spilled oil spreads across the surface of sea water. It forms a thin layer called an oil slick.

OIL FACT

More than 2,700 million litres of oil seep into the oceans every year.

oil spill accident that releases oil into the environment

environment natural world of land, water, and air

Oil and the environment

Oil in sea water sticks to living things, such as shellfish and crabs. Fish that feed on these animals take in the oil. The fish may become ill or die.

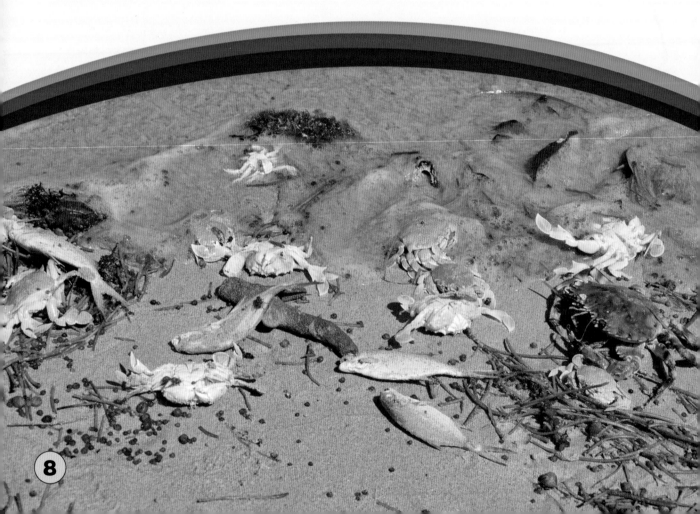

On beaches, oil sticks to sand and rocks.
It washes into **wetlands** and sinks into the
soil. Plants take in the oil through their roots.
The oil damages the plants. It also harms
animals that eat the plants.

wetland area of land that is sometimes covered by water

Oil-covered animals

Oil covers animals' fur and feathers. This coating makes it hard for them to swim or fly. The animals may even become ill when they try to clean oil off their bodies. Oil can also cover young birds in their nests and kill them.

OIL FACT

Thick oil can also coat birds' eggs. It can stop the eggs from hatching.

Battered ships

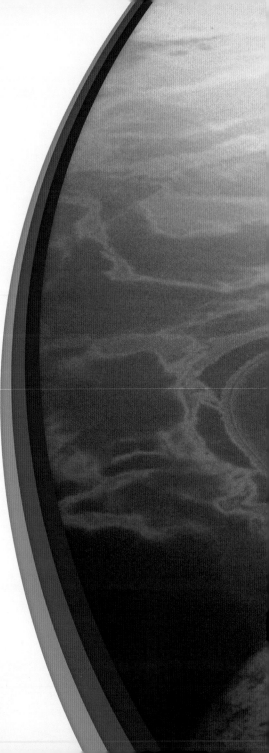

Many spills happen when ships carrying oil are damaged. In 1989, the *Exxon Valdez* hit land in shallow water.

The ship broke open and spilled oil into Prince William Sound in Alaska, USA. The spill was one of the worst in history. The oil slick stretched over 750 kilometres.

It had a terrible effect on wildlife in the area. It is thought to have killed around 250,000 sea birds, nearly 3,000 sea otters, 300 harbour seals, 250 bald eagles, and 22 killer whales. It is still affecting plants and animals today.

Offshore oil rigs

An oil rig is a platform built in the ocean to drill for oil. Oil rig accidents can quickly spill thousands of barrels of oil.

In April 2010, an explosion happened at an oil rig known as *Deepwater Horizon*. Oil gushed from a well on the ocean floor for nearly three months. Soon, oil reached coastlines all along the Gulf of Mexico in the USA.

Cleaning up the mess

One way people contain oil spills is with **booms**. A boom is like a fence that is put into the water. Booms stop the oil from spreading. Most booms are filled with air. Others are filled with hair, fur, or feathers.

boom

boom tube-like structure that floats on water and stops oil from spreading

skimmer

A boom gathers oil into one area.
Boats with machines called skimmers
then remove oil from the water. A skimmer
works like a vacuum cleaner for water.

Every little helps

Emergency workers help to clean up oil that reaches coastlines. They hose down rocks and sand to help clean off the oil. They rake soil and clean animals.

Emergency workers sometimes spray special **bacteria** on the oil to help speed up the cleaning process. The bacteria feed on the oil and help to break it down over time.

emergency worker person who helps
at emergencies
bacteria tiny living creatures that feed on
things around them

19

Saving wildlife

Emergency workers can help to save birds that are covered in oil.

1

Workers rescue, feed, and warm a bird.

2

They give the oily bird lots of bubble baths.

3 Warm air dryers help the bird's feathers get back to normal.

4 The clean, healthy bird is released into a safe environment.

Other animals such as dolphins and sea turtles are also at risk from oil spills. Emergency workers and other helpers work hard to try and save them, but many do not survive.

OIL FACT

It can take up to 1,136 litres of water to clean the oil from just one pelican. That is enough water to fill over 14 bathtubs!

Glossary

bacteria tiny living creatures that feed on things around them

boom tube-like structure that floats on water and stops oil from spreading

emergency worker person who helps at emergencies

environment natural world of land, water, and air

natural resource material people use that is found in nature

oil spill accident that releases oil into the environment

petroleum thick, oily liquid found below Earth's surface

wetland area of land that is sometimes covered by water

Find out more

Books

The Exxon Valdez's Deadly Oil Spill (Code Red), Linda Beech (Bearport, 2007)

Sea Otter Rescue: The Aftermath of an Oil Spill, Roland Smith (Puffin, 1999)

Sinister Sludge: Oil Spills and the Environment (Jr. Graphic Environmental Dangers), Daniel R. Faust (Powerkids Press, 2009)

Internet sites

kidsblogs.nationalgeographic.com/greenscene/gulf-oil-spill.html
Visit this website for information about the 2010 oil spill in the Gulf of Mexico. Test your memory with a fun quiz.

news.bbc.co.uk/cbbcnews/hi/newsid_8650000/newsid_8659800/8659836.stm
You can view pictures of the 2010 oil spill on this website. Click on the links on the right to find information and videos about other oil spills.

Index

With thanks to my family and friends, who always get me through these Herculean endeavours. Thanks for the late nights, the burnout and the support. Thank you to Rob Cooper for his technical review and a thank you to my friends at CG. And with infinite gratitude to my editor – without all the effort, this couldn't happen.

First published 2018 by Walker Books Ltd
87 Vauxhall Walk, London SE11 5HJ

2 4 6 8 10 9 7 5 3 1

Text © 2018 David Whitney
Illustrations © 2018 Duncan Beedie

The right of David Whitney and Duncan Beedie to be identified as author and illustrator respectively of this work has been asserted by them in accordance with the Copyright, Designs and Patents Act 1988

This book has been typeset in Futura and Bokka

Printed in China

British Library Cataloguing in Publication Data:
a catalogue record for this book is available from the British Library

ISBN 978-1-4063-8249-5

www.walker.co.uk
www.getcodingkids.com